The
HAPPIEST SONG
PLAYS LAST

THE ELLIOT PLAYS
BY QUIARA ALEGRÍA HUDES
PUBLISHED BY TCG

INCLUDES:

Elliot, A Soldier's Fugue
Water by the Spoonful
The Happiest Song Plays Last

The

HAPPIEST SONG
PLAYS LAST

Quiara Alegría Hudes

THEATRE COMMUNICATIONS GROUP
NEW YORK
2014

The Happiest Song Plays Last is published by Theatre Communications Group, Inc., 520 Eighth Avenue, 24th Floor, New York, NY 10018-4156

The publication of *The Happiest Song Plays Last* by Quiara Alegría Hudes, through TCG's Book Program, is made possible in part by the New York State Council on the Arts with the support of Governor Andrew Cuomo and the New York State Legislature.

Special thanks to The Joyce Foundation for its generous support of this publication.

TCG books are exclusively distributed to the book trade by Consortium Book Sales and Distribution.

LIBRARY OF CONGRESS CATALOGING-IN-PUBLICATION DATA
Hudes, Quiara Alegría.
The happiest song plays last / Quiara Alegría Hudes.
pages cm
ISBN 978-1-55936-446-1 (paperback)
ISBN 978-1-55936-463-8 (trade cloth)
ISBN 978-1-55936-772-1 (ebook)
1. Iraq War, 2003-2011—Veterans—Drama. 2. Self-realization—Drama. 3. Jordan—Drama. I. Title.
PS3608.U3234H37   2014
812'.6—dc23   2014015935

Book design and composition by Lisa Govan
Cover design by Rodrigo Corral & Joan Wong

First Edition, November 2014
Second Printing, March 2022

For Virginia and Sedo Sanchez
—Mom and Pop—
who blasted Ramito
way too early in the morning

Acknowledgments

I am marrow-deep grateful to Elliot Ruiz—my cousin, my muse, my inspiration. When he returned from Iraq that boyish sparkle in his eye had changed, ever so slightly. As his life story continued to unfold I continued to write and Elliot gave me his blessing and took my creative license in stride.

Yaz's press conference statement is based on a speech written by Roger Zepernick. With his permission I have adapted it here.

Though fictional, this play is inspired by two real events: Joaquín Rivera's experience at the Aria Health Clinic in Philadelphia in 2009 and the filming of the movie *Battle for Haditha.*

The following people gave of their spirit and stories in interviews: Nelson González on the history and essence of the music, and Nilda Ruiz and Maria Quiñones-Sanchez with tales of Joaquín the guidance counselor and neighbor. Danielle Allen, Najla Said, Ryan Shams, Rohina Malik and Kareem Fahim shared candid points of view.

My collaborators. Five actors gathered at New Dramatists as this play was born: Andrea Burns, Demosthenes Chrysan,

Mateo Gomez, Armando Riesco and Najla Said. The family grew at the Eugene O'Neill Theater Center: Eddie Torres, Zabryna Guevara, Jaime Tirelli, Kevin Geer. In Chicago, more joined the circle: James Harms, Sandra Marquez, Fawzia Mirza, Demetrios Troy. Finally, Ruben Santiago-Hudson brought it all home with Dariush Kashani, Anthony Chilsholm, Lauren Vélez, Tony Plana and Annapurna Sriram. I am grateful to each and every one of them, but one name bears repeating: Armando, you fought with me to the very end—we were fighting for the same thing, and we got there, and I cherish that.

My champions. Tanya Palmer, the entire Goodman Theatre, the Joyce Foundation. Carole Rothman and Second Stage Theatre. John Beinecke and Page 73 Productions.

My family. In particular: my aunt Linda Hudes, my mother Virginia Sanchez, and my children Cecilia and Julian Beauchamp.

My husband, my friend, my most dedicated dramaturg: Ray Beauchamp.

There have been great changes in the face of the country, in its levels and contour, and in the direction and beds of its water-courses since the days of the Swedes and the early Quakers. Some streams have disappeared, some have changed their direction, nearly all have been reduced in volume and depth . . . in the building of a great city.

—J. THOMAS SCHARF AND THOMPSON WESTCOTT,
History of Philadelphia

The

HAPPIEST SONG
PLAYS LAST

Production History

The Happiest Song Plays Last had its world premiere at the
Goodman Theatre (Robert Falls, Artistic Director; Roche
Schulfer, Executive Director) in Chicago on April 22, 2013.
It was directed by Edward Torres. The set design was by Col-
lette Pollard, the costume design was by Christine Pascual,
the lighting design was by Jesse Klug, the sound design was
by Ray Nardelli and Joshua Horvath, the original music was
by Nelson González and the projection design was by John
Boesche; the dramaturg was Tanya Palmer and the production stage manager was Kimberly Osgood. The cast was:

ELLIOT	Armando Riesco
YAZ	Sandra Marquez
SHAR	Fawzia Mirza
AGUSTÍN	Jaime Tirelli
ALI	Demetrios Troy
LEFTY	James Harms
MUSICIAN	Nelson González

The Happiest Song Plays Last had its New York premiere at
Second Stage Theatre (Carole Rothman, Artistic Director;
Casey Reitz, Executive Director) on March 3, 2014. It was
directed by Ruben Santiago-Hudson. The set design was by

Michael Carnahan, the costume design was by Karen Perry, the lighting design was by Rui Rita, the sound design was by Leon Rothenberg and the original music was by Nelson González; the production stage manager was Amanda Michaels. The cast was:

ELLIOT	Armando Riesco
YAZ	Lauren Vélez
SHAR	Annapurna Sriram
AGUSTÍN	Tony Plana
ALI	Dariush Kashani
LEFTY	Anthony Chisholm
THE MUSICIANS	Nelson González
	Nelson Jaime
	John Rodriguez

Characters

ELLIOT, Latino, twenties

YAZ, Latina, Elliot's cousin, thirties

SHAR, short for Shahrnush, Arab-American, emphasis on the American, twenties

AGUSTÍN, Latino, sixties

ALI, Arab, thick accent, forties

LEFTY, any ethnicity—he's a cultural "outsider" to the community but fits right in, forties–seventies

The Musicians

The cuatro is Puerto Rico's national instrument, much like the guitar but with a metallic twang. This play will benefit from a trio of live musicians: a guitar player, a cuatro player and a bongo/güiro player, at least one of whom should sing. If possible, the cuatro player might learn to play oud, or learn/adapt oud repertoire on the cuatro. If three musicians are not possible, a single live guitarist/vocalist will still be beautiful. If no live music is possible, please research recordings of Puerto Rican classics, Ramito being my personal favorite.

SETTING

January–February 2011, then a year later. Philadelphia and various locations in Jordan.

PROLOGUE

A traditional lyric says: On the mountain plantations of Puerto Rico, stoking a wood stove, pulling a wobbly plow, with a fresh breeze, and hand-picked root vegetables, in a house too small for a TV, with windows too narrow for air conditioners, miles from the highway, that one might live better than a millionaire.

In the performance space, the Musicians play, pulling the wobbly plow of memory back to a verdant day that perhaps we remember ourselves, or perhaps we only remember our parents' remembering.

Act One

SCENE 1

The Film Set of *Haditha on Fire*. Azraq, Jordan. January 2011.

A violent explosion. The sound of debris landing in the explosion's wake. Shar, in a traditional abaya, lies on the ground. She is harnessed for flying.

SHAR: Oh shit . . . Ow . . . Uhhhh . . .

(*Elliot enters in combat gear, fake blood.*)

ELLIOT: Yoooooo! You flew! You fucking trampolined! You okay? Shar? Shar! You good?
SHAR: Aw . . . That hurt. Ow.
ELLIOT: Who are you where are you?
SHAR: I'm Shar. I'm in Jordan filming a movie.
ELLIOT (*Holding up fingers*): Count.
SHAR: Three. I think I'm okay . . . Ugh . . .

ELLIOT: Breathe, dude. Get up slowly.

SHAR: What happened?

ELLIOT: The second they said action, this gust of wind came up, you could literally see the air moving. That thing detonated sixty degrees to the left! Even Nigel was running cuz he was like, "Protect the cameras! Protect the film!"

SHAR (*Spitting*): I have a mouthful of pebbles.

ELLIOT: Shit looked tight.

SHAR: Yeah?

ELLIOT: You trampolined like twenty feet off the ground!

(*Shar has made it to her feet. Elliot removes the harness from her.*)

SHAR: I hope he got what he needs.

ELLIOT: Don't worry, he doesn't have another bomb. I told that hardhead of his. This is the desert. This ain't no soundstage. You can't manipulate an explosion when you got wind like this. On the ride out here, I saw that grass blowing all around, I was like, "Nigel, man, the weather conditions aren't right."

SHAR: We better get credit for these stunts.

ELLIOT: Docudrama. Everything's gotta be real.

SHAR: FYI, a stunt in Hollywood is falling to your knees.

ELLIOT: FYI, I been knowed that.

SHAR (*Snapping her fingers near her ear*): I'm gonna go deaf for an indie. For no distribution.

ELLIOT: We're gonna be distributed.

SHAR: The optimistic newbie.

ELLIOT: Don't you believe in The Secret? Manifest it.

SHAR: Manifest me a soft mattress to lie on.

ELLIOT: I ain't no newbie. National Colgate ad.

SHAR: You sent me the link to that ad three times.

ELLIOT: National Target ad, bee-yotch.

SHAR: I stand humbled, Sidney Poitier.

ELLIOT: We can't all go to the Yale School of Drama.

SHAR: Juilliard.

(Ali enters, rushes to Shar.)

ALI: My sister, my sister!

SHAR: It looked jacked, didn't it?

ALI: Beautiful, beautiful. You are a bird!

SHAR: I need to shower.

ALI: Nigel says you fall down wrong way. They have to make explosion again. They send car to next town to buy new explosion.

SHAR: No!

ELLIOT: How far is the next town?

ALI: Thirty minutes.

(Shar pulls cigarettes from her abaya.)

SHAR *(To Ali)*: Smoke?

ALI: No, my sister.

SHAR: Suit yourself, Little Mr. Innocent.

ELLIOT: Don't act like I didn't walk in on you with porn jacking off last night.

ALI: Please, my brother! *(To Shar)* This is not true.

SHAR: All right, Ali. I like you more than I realized.

ALI *(Regarding the cigarettes)*: Okay, I take one for my uncle.

(Shar gives him a cigarette. Ali guards it in his pocket.)

ELLIOT: Something was off with the timing. Listen, before the bomb goes off, like four seconds after they call action, the Humvee's gonna come around the corner, and when I go into the house, that's when you get in ready position. When the ropes pull you up, suck in your abs for the liftoff.

SHAR: Did they train you in flying trapeze in the Marines?

ELLIOT: Yeah, just like they trained you to shit diamonds at Yale.

SHAR AND ELLIOT: Juilliard.

ELLIOT: And don't forget, flip backward.

SHAR: I did!

ELLIOT: You flipped forward, Juilliard.

SHAR: I thought I flipped backward.

(Pause.)

So is the real thing actually like this? An IED blows and people become aerialists above the road?

ELLIOT: People? I seen Bradleys, I seen tanks flipping like Sea World dolphins. From a *medium* explosion like this one.

SHAR *(To Ali)*: This punk is telling me that was a medium explosion. That in approximately thirty minutes I'm going to get my butt killed by a medium explosion.

ELLIOT: Not if you clench those abs.

ALI: I see explosions, too. Same like Elliot. This is medium.

ELLIOT: Your scream was on point.

SHAR: I pissed my abaya.

ALI: You need new abaya? I go talk to wardrobe.

SHAR: That's not your job.

ALI: Yes. This morning Nigel fires assistant, says, "Ali, you want second job?" Official: Now I am Consultant on Arab Culture *and* Number One Gofer.

ELLIOT: Congratulations. You moving down in the world, bro!

ALI: But never as low as you, my lovely. One minute. No problemo. *(Exits)*

SHAR: Hey everything okay?

ELLIOT: Hells yeah.

SHAR: I saw you last night. Three in the morning, outside.

ELLIOT: I don't . . .

SHAR: Digging in the dirt, it looked like you were shaking or something was wrong.

ELLIOT *(Lying)*: Hm, wasn't me. Must have been one of the other guys. *(Upbeat)* Hey, our first scene together.

SHAR: Crazy that I'm shooting it with *you.*

ELLIOT: You think Rob's back in L.A. by now?

SHAR: I've never seen a lead actor get fired. Two weeks into filming? So what went down?

ELLIOT: Stupid shit.

SHAR: Come on.

ELLIOT: Just a lot of stupidity.

SHAR: I admire your discretion.

ELLIOT: He flew in two weeks late.

SHAR: Eh he he he.

ELLIOT: I had to give him his own separate boot camp from what I gave all the other guys cuz it's in his contract. All the other actors playing Marines get a two-week boot camp. I grind them down so they know how it is, out in the field. Rob gets a luxury three-day boot camp. So day one I'm giving him the basics, a few drills and he has his band members and his girlfriend watching, smacking their gum and drinking fuckin' Fanta out of straws like we're at the movies.

SHAR: We are at the movies.

ELLIOT: I'm like, how did they even get to Jordan is what I want to know.

SHAR: Their flights were in his contract.

ELLIOT: After boot camp day one, I was like, he can't cut it. I showed the guys to do this thing with their voice, that it's gotta come from down here.

SHAR: The diaphragm.

ELLIOT: Like, *(Imitating a Marine screaming)* "HEY!" I'm trying to show him how to do it, he's like, *(A film whisper)* "Hey." I'm like, no man, you do that in the Marines, you do that when a chopper's overhead and you got open fire? No one will hear you! Your ass just got zapped by a haji. It's gotta be, "HEY!" Then he just didn't bother showing up for boot camp day two. Day three I'm over it. I'm supposed to give him his haircut.

SHAR: Oh man, he was piiiiiiissed!

ELLIOT: So I have the clippers. He was like, "Not too much. Leave at least an inch." I went in a straight line down the middle with the clippers. *(Makes the clipper sound)* He looked in the mirror and started screaming, "What the fuck?! What the fuck?! Does this look like an inch off the top to you?!" I was like, motherfucker, I *knew* you could use your diaphragm!

SHAR: But how'd you get the role? Monday morning you're the research assistant, an hour later you're in wardrobe?

ELLIOT: Like Nigel's not riding me hard enough already. *(As Nigel—a British accent)* "Oh yes, I want a shot up there with the Marines running into the sunset." *(As himself)* "Nigel, Marines don't do that." *(As Nigel)* "Elliot, relax, pull the stick from your asshole." *(As himself)* "Nigel, in the history of war not a single Marine has ever run into the fucking sunset." After a few days of filming Nigel starts blaming me that his lead actor sucks. He's like, "Elliot, didn't you train him? Elliot, what the fuck? Did you give him the boot camp or not?" I told him plain, I was like, "Nigel, he can't cut it. He's not convincing as a Marine in a leadership position." Nigel's like, *(Sighs)* "Fine, we'll send him home and re-shoot everything with you as the lead."

SHAR: Holy crap! Were you like, "What?!"

ELLIOT: I called my agent. She was like, "Hells yeah, we're gonna get you a point!" I ain't even know what a point was. She was like, "It's back end. It's a piece of the pie."

SHAR: Hold on, you got a point?

ELLIOT: No. Nigel was like, "Elliot, what the fuck is going on? Your agent thinks she's a big badass but she isn't. Do you want to do it or not?" I was like, "Pay her ten percent and let's do it."

SHAR: So wait, you're not getting paid at all?

ELLIOT: Oh, I'm getting paid. How much are you getting?

SHAR: How much are *you* getting?

(Ali enters with a dry abaya.)

ALI: Clean abaya.

SHAR: Thanks, Ali.

(Shar changes into the dry abaya.)

ALI: No problem, my friend. *(Lighting the cigarette, smoking)* For my uncle.

SHAR: My underwear's still wet.

ALI: You need dry underwear?

SHAR: Wardrobe ran out yesterday.

ELLIOT: Just like the Marines.

(Ali gets a text, reads it.)

ALI: Nigel must find two more bombs. Day off tomorrow.

SHAR: Thank god.

ELLIOT: Hells yeah! Egypt! Say it with me, Ali, Egypt!

ALI: It is not possible. You need two days for Egypt in peaceful time and I cannot take you. You hire different driver for Egypt.

ELLIOT: Valley of the Kings, Karnak Temple. Your suggestions.

ALI: This suggestion was last week, before Tahrir Square is full of protest, before roads are blocked.

ELLIOT: Shit, I'd like to see those protests, too.

SHAR: You're weird.

ELLIOT: People marching in the street so they can vote? Yo, give me a sign, I'll join right in.

SHAR: My dad called at three A.M., "Egypt is on fire! They're beheading mummies in the museum, come home!" I was like, Dad, I'm in Jordan, breathe.

ALI: Do you see bridge photograph? Ten thousand protestors praying on bridge over Nile. Teenage boy holds Egyptian flag, police put water cannon at boy's face, but still, boy holds flag.

SHAR: What news site do you use?

ALI: Facebook. You have internet on phone?

(Shar hands Ali her phone. He types, shows her the page.)

Good page. Protest organizer.

SHAR *(Looking)*: "When you arrive at Tahrir Square tonight do not provoke the infantry. No screaming, throwing or insults. Hug a soldier. Bring your sons and daughters, have your child hug the soldier, too. They will not shoot the protestors if they are part of the protestors."

ELLIOT: That's what's up.

SHAR: Can a gal from Beverly Hills friend the Egyptian revolution?

ELLIOT: Join them. March with them.

SHAR: How? We're two countries away.

(Elliot opens his arms wide.)

ELLIOT: But there's a soldier right here. "Hug a soldier tonight, baby."

SHAR: I'm good.

(Elliot takes the phone, clicks a button.)

ELLIOT: There. You just friended them.

ALI: Congratulations. You are revolutionary! I am, too.

ELLIOT: All right, tomorrow. Day off. Name the destination. Name the price. And not some rinky-dink shit. I don't want to see the fuckin' McDonald's in Amman.

ALI: Tomorrow, I show you real Jordan. You come to my house, meet my wife and mother-in-law. You have taste of araq?

ELLIOT: That liquor? Are you allowed to drink that?

ALI: Not for me. I have araq for special guests. We go very early to my house, you have early lunch, then we drive south. I take you to Petra. Beautiful. Architecture better than Guggenheim museum, better than scientist can build. Then drive all day to Dead Sea, very salty, you can float on top and hold newspaper to read it. Jordan is the most beautiful country.

ELLIOT: I'm in. Shar?

SHAR: You don't have to spend your free time showing us around.

ALI: Not free time, work time. You give me money for gas, a little extra for family.

SHAR: I promised my dad I'd stay on set.

ELLIOT: What Daddy don't know won't kill him.

ALI: I show you that you are my American sister. You see my wife's hair. Beautiful, wavy. She takes off hijab, like family.

SCENE 2

Yaz's House. North Philadelphia. January 2011.

Just before sunrise. A small, cramped kitchen and dining area in a crumbling part of Philly. Modest architecture, but glowing with life and an artsy style. A door leads out to the adjacent abandoned lot that's been turned into a garden oasis—though right now it's a frozen January oasis.

On the stove, pots are stacked two and three high, bubbling. Yaz and Agustín enter.

AGUSTÍN: The whole city of Philadelphia can smell it!

YAZ: What? Your breath?

AGUSTÍN: Your kitchen.

YAZ: Because your breath smacked me in the face the second I stepped foot in the courtroom.

AGUSTÍN *(Playful, sniffs)*: Arroz junto con Vienna sausage . . . *(Sniffs)* On the side, pink beans . . . *(Sniffs)* And in the pink beans you didn't put potato, you put calabaza.

YAZ: Don't touch a pot. Don't so much as touch a spoon.

AGUSTÍN: I hate jail. Thirty people, one toilet, no food.

YAZ: Then stop going there.

AGUSTÍN: If there was someone else I could have called, I would.

YAZ: You have a wife. Her name is Miriam.

AGUSTÍN: Best friends are less judgmental.

YAZ: Next time my phone rings at five in the morning I will not answer. You hear me, Agustín? .16? I went to college. I partied. I know what blood alcohol level .16 is.

AGUSTÍN: This winter is killing me.

YAZ: Ay. Frame your excuses and hang them on a wall. You'll fill a whole damn museum!

AGUSTÍN: I go house to house playing cuatro all night, my fingers get cold, they need to be warmed up or I can't play. I was saying to the güiro player, "Ramon, my fingers are stiff as remote controls!"

YAZ: I texted Ramon twice after I left the parranda. "Don't let Agustín drink. And do not let him drive home."

AGUSTÍN: It just felt so good to be playing again. After all this snow, after every parranda got snowed out? Comay, these three months are all we get. Thanksgiving to Las Octavitas, then we sit on our hands the rest of the year. So when last night didn't get cancelled? The only holiday party we were able to play all season?

YAZ: Do you know how many strings Joe had to pull? The judges he had to wake up so you could be here right now?

AGUSTÍN: A lawyer with a heart out to here. I tried to pay the man and he wouldn't take the money.

YAZ: He didn't need your twenty dollars.

(Yaz finds a Sharpie. She grabs Agustín's wrist, writes a dot on the face of his watch.)

AGUSTÍN: Oye . . . Yazmin! You give me a watch and then you destroy it?

YAZ: Call me after that dot, you're going straight to voice mail. Next time I won't call Joe. I'll let that judge slap you with ninety days.

AGUSTÍN: You used to call me a hero when they cuffed me and took me in.

YAZ: For protesting the bombing in Vieques, Agustín, not for passing out on the shoulder of Roosevelt Boulevard.

AGUSTÍN: Yazmin, you think it was fun waking up, not knowing where I was, a cop tapping on my window?

YAZ: Ay, I taught all day . . . I have a faculty meeting at eight A.M. . . . cooking all night . . . getting your call . . .

AGUSTÍN: I'll rub your feet.

YAZ: First look at the garden. I'm gonna set you up to play next to the jacaranda. You see those blue flowers?

AGUSTÍN: In the winter? How'd you do it?

YAZ: It lives upstairs in the bathtub. I turn on the shower, they perk up in the humidity. They pop up like fireworks, that fast. Like little trumpets to the sky. And the güiro vine?

AGUSTÍN: A güiro vine in January!

YAZ: You should see the upstairs tub. There's hardly room for me to wash my hair. Oye, yesterday morning I brought the güiro vine down and put it outside. The dirt was frozen solid, I had to pickax a hole. I put the roots in, arranged the vine all over the wall. When I got home from teaching—I saw someone hop the gate, with two of my güiros under his arm! Because they look that good. I chased him down with a broom. I said, "Give me those! And come to my Three Kings parranda on Friday." Ave Maria, this neighborhood is like an old Victorian home. You have to live in it while you fix it up. Never in a million years did I think I'd be living on these blocks, but here I am trying to fix everyone's craziness. *(Sitting)* You have permission to rub my feet. If you tell me a story.

(He rubs her feet.)

AGUSTÍN: The biggest fiesta in my family was the day we got a radio. My aunt had a table just for that radio. Nothing else would go on that table! When we heard that cuatro music over the radio for the first time? Wow! We knew we were important! All the jíbaros learned each other's styles. They would be imitating each other, competing with each other.

YAZ: Does your wife wait for you?

AGUSTÍN: When?

YAZ: When you stay late running at the mouth.

AGUSTÍN: It's already morning.

YAZ: Sun hasn't risen.

AGUSTÍN: I'm having a conversation with a friend, why does she care?

(A knock at the door.)

YAZ: Come in! It's open!

(Another knock.)

It's Lefty. I know his knock. IT'S OPEN! He refuses to open the door himself.

(She gets up and opens the door. Lefty is there. He is a possibly old, somehow ageless homeless man with luminous eyes. His pockets are stuffed full of miscellaneous possessions. He keeps his gaze fixed firmly to the ground.

He uses the word "mom" as a term of endearment for Yaz, similar to "ma'am.")

LEFTY: Hi, mom.

YAZ: You don't knock on my door for a week? Where have you been?

LEFTY: Directing traffic, mom.

YAZ: Well you're still in one piece so that deserves a plate of food, don't you think?

LEFTY: It smells like chicken and macaroni.

YAZ *(Pointing to the stove)*: That pot's yours. I knew you were coming today. Eat what you want, take the rest with you.

LEFTY: Look at those pots, mom. Stacked up like building blocks.

YAZ *(Pointing to a pot)*: That pot is for Doña Manza's grand-kids. *(Pointing to another one)* Pasteles for the blind woman on the corner. Her home-care person just got deported. *(Pointing to another pot)* One pot of soup for Miguelito's boy in the hospital.

AGUSTÍN: They still got that kid on all those machines?

YAZ: Last time I brought him soup his IV line was clogged all the way back into the bag. Go to that hospital, you just get sicker.

AGUSTÍN: Verdad.

YAZ *(Back to Lefty, pointing)*: And I got four pots on there for the Three Kings party. Friday night. You're coming, right?

(Lefty nods, serves himself. Yaz returns to her foot rub.)

AGUSTÍN: Do you have to leave your doors unlocked?

YAZ: Open door, open stove.

AGUSTÍN: People know you're here alone.

YAZ: He's never given me any trouble. Lefty, you need some work? It's supposed to be clear tomorrow. No rain. Wanna help me pour some cement in the backyard?

LEFTY: I have to direct traffic, mom.

YAZ: We'll be done by noon.

LEFTY: But cement doesn't work.

YAZ: Doesn't work for what?

LEFTY: For covering up the river.

YAZ *(Perplexed)*: I'm not covering anything, I'm fixing the patio for my holiday party.

LEFTY: The cement just cracks.

YAZ: What are you talking about?

LEFTY: Miss Ginny told me about the river. Remember her?

YAZ: She was my aunt.

LEFTY: She lived here.

YAZ: Yes, Lefty.

LEFTY: She was my mom before she died and then you became my mom. She told me about the rivers down there. Holding up the city like a bobbin when you go fishing. One time a whole block of houses sunk into it.

AGUSTÍN: That's right, up in Kensington. *(To Yaz)* Before you were born. They were swallowed up like quicksand. Cheap construction, they didn't build the foundations right.

LEFTY: Greenmount Cemetery is on top of a river, too.

AGUSTÍN: I sing at those graves every Mother's Day. Never seen no river.

LEFTY: This house is on top of one, too. She said that's why the garden grows so nice. She said a thousand years ago there were only streams and Indians. That's why the sidewalk has so many cracks. Because the river tries to come back up again.

YAZ *(To Agustín)*: That's the most I've ever heard him talk. *(To Lefty)* Lefty. I'll give you dinner for a month if you help me pour the concrete.

LEFTY: I'll be here when the sun rises.

(Lefty eats in silence. Agustín has a sudden cramp in his arm.)

AGUSTÍN: Ay . . . Ay dios mio. Damn!

YAZ: You all right?

AGUSTÍN: It's your callouses. They give me arm cramps.

YAZ: My callouses? Your fingers are like sandpaper.

(He has another arm cramp.)

AGUSTÍN: All week when I play, it just cramps up like this. Ay . . . Ave Maria . . .

YAZ: It's that carpel tunnel. When's the last time you had it looked at?

AGUSTÍN: I'm an old man.

YAZ: Ay, here we go!

AGUSTÍN: All my upper teeth are implants.

YAZ: I have two porcelain caps, so? Quit boozing, you'll grow ten years younger.

AGUSTÍN: I got no kids, Yaz, no legacy. What will I leave behind?

YAZ: Your niece and nephew.

AGUSTÍN: They don't have my direct blood. My DNA. I was sitting in that jail cell tonight thinking, What the hell are you doing with your life, muchacho? I'm a man without a child.

YAZ: Your nephew became a doctor. Your niece is an engineer. How many students did you help get into college last year? Out of the roughest high school in this city?

AGUSTÍN: And how many of them have already dropped out? Or flunked out?

YAZ: How many free music lessons do you give every day? How many five year olds have you taught to play the cuatro? Like my cousin Elliot, you're his role model.

AGUSTÍN: Stories fade. Songs disappear. But not blood.

YAZ: What does Miriam have to say about it?

AGUSTÍN: Yazmin, this isn't easy for me.

YAZ: What?

AGUSTÍN: I'm ashamed.

YAZ: Ashamed of what?

AGUSTÍN: God knows I've never asked anyone for a penny, for a single favor.

YAZ: Favor?

AGUSTÍN: I know I'm twice your age.

YAZ: Whoa. Hold on.

AGUSTÍN: I was your first music teacher. Before Yale University discovered you.

YAZ: Agustín, I didn't know you felt that way about me.

AGUSTÍN: You got good DNA, meng. La Profesora! You're a professor of music. You sing Mozart in your sleep. Carajo, when you sneeze it sounds like Beethoven. You don't have the barrio mentality. You've got one toe in this neighborhood and nine toes out in the rest of the world.

YAZ: Are you out of your mind?

AGUSTÍN: Just because you're divorced doesn't mean you can't have a family. You feed a hundred people a week. What's one more mouth? One more mouth that you made.

YAZ: This viejo is dead serious! *(A moment. Then)* Are you serious? *(A moment)* This block is my children. This neighborhood is all the dysfunctional family I need.

AGUSTÍN: And what brought you here? How'd you decide to buy this house? You were living in a penthouse in Center City.

YAZ: What does that have to do with this?

AGUSTÍN: How'd you decide? You've told me a hundred times.

YAZ: It was impulsive. Aunt Ginny died and a bell rang in my heart. Just "ding" and, "Oh, I have to go fix up Ginny's house . . ."

AGUSTÍN: Was it part of your grand plan?

YAZ: No . . .

AGUSTÍN: Ding! Your eyes just lit up like two sapphires.

YAZ: Oh my god . . . *(She sits)* Rub my foot. *(He does)* I mean this neighborhood is no place to raise kids. Take care of others' kids, maybe . . . And you're no gem. Alcoholism runs in the blood, it's genetic, it's a proclivity . . . And what about Miriam? She's my neighbor. I look the woman in the eye every day.

AGUSTÍN: Every day?

YAZ: I see the woman. We both shop at Sanchez Grocery!

AGUSTÍN: We haven't officially been together for years.

YAZ: Do you share a bed?

AGUSTÍN: We can't afford another bed, and there's no room in the house for it anyway. We grew cold a long time ago.

YAZ: My life is in two parts. Before this foot rub and after this foot rub.

AGUSTÍN: Ha ha!

YAZ: Don't you celebrate. You just messed up all my plans! Lefty?

LEFTY: Yes, mom?

YAZ: I know you're listening. Don't play innocent. What should I do?

LEFTY: You're the best mother in the whole world.

YAZ: Holy shit . . .

AGUSTÍN: Ha ha! I know where I'm from. I know who I am. Now I know where I'm going.

YAZ: No one knows where they're going.

AGUSTÍN: When I die, I'm going out with a smile on my face, laughing, like this! *(Laughs)*

SCENE 3

Texting.

Elliot and Yaz typing.

YAZ: Haven't slept 2 days straight. 3 Kings party tmrw.

ELLIOT: 3 kings? on jan 29?

YAZ: Xmas eve, Xmas, and 3 Kings got snowed out this year. Parties delayed. I will serve u big plate of food, take picture, email it to u.

ELLIOT: i hatechu, cousin food talk strictly forbiden

YAZ: I cook bistec, the meat melts on contact with tongue. sooooo soft.

ELLIOT: yeah ill think of that next time i bite into a shawarma

YAZ: Shawarma?

ELLIOT: basically an arab burrito

YAZ: Read about Cairo this morning.

ELLIOT: crazy, film crew is excited

YAZ: They're airlifting americans the f out of there. U safe?

ELLIOT: egypt is 2 countries away

YAZ: World is changing and youre in arms reach. I miss your mom, If she heard about a protest she'd drop everything.

ELLIOT: arizona 2009?

YAZ: Womans in remission, hops a grayhound to go march with los mexicanos.

ELLIOT: out here tryin to make her memory proud. gotta run, off to petra

YAZ: ps. I like a boy.

ELLIOT: WhAT?????!!!!!???

YAZ: logoff

SCENE 4

Ali's House. Jerash, Jordan.

Elliot and Shar sit on the floor, looking down at a plate of meat.
They are dressed in casual western clothes—jeans and T-shirts.

SHAR: Wow.

ELLIOT: I don't think that happens every day.

SHAR: It's just hair. But my heart was pounding.

ELLIOT: Why does he trust us so much? Invites us into his home.

SHAR: His wife and daughter are so pretty.

ELLIOT: Those hazel eyes?

SHAR: Without the scarf the person looks so different.

ELLIOT: I would never have gotten the chance to do any of this . . .

SHAR: If it weren't for the movie?

ELLIOT: Did you ever have the feeling . . . that you might get to close a chapter in your life?

29

SHAR: Did you ever have the feeling that you're cracking open the book of your life? The walk here? This versus California? Everything I take for granted at home?

ELLIOT: Jerash is one old-ass city.

SHAR: Roman ruins? I had no idea, my jaw almost fell to the ground.

ELLIOT: "Yo, Ali, what's that?" "Roman ruins, my brother." "Yo, Ali, is that Roman ruins, too?" "No, my brother, this is shitty abandoned boys school."

SHAR: I feel terrible even thinking this but . . .

ELLIOT: Say it.

SHAR: It's a shithole.

ELLIOT: It looks like Stella Street. Collapsed buildings, diagonal walls.

SHAR: Where's Stella Street?

ELLIOT: North Philly. Block where I was born. A little different than the block you're from?

SHAR: Cul-de-sac. Full-regulation croquet court in my backyard. No one around who looked anything like me.

ELLIOT: I don't mean this any type of way, but how come you speak Arabic on camera but not with Ali or the crew?

SHAR: I learned in college, thought I'd land more roles. It was a career investment. I never spoke at home.

ELLIOT: We didn't speak English at home. So in high school? When I flunked Intro to Spanish? My moms was like, "Damn Elliot, can't you speak your own language?"

SHAR: I'm one-quarter Egyptian, one-quarter Iranian, with Cherokee, Korean and WASP thrown in for flavor. People are like, "What are you?" I look 'em square in the eye and say, "Nothing."

ELLIOT: Nothing?

SHAR: I could spend twenty-four-seven explaining what I am to people and they still won't get it.

ELLIOT: My local school, they make every kid feel like nothing. They got that shit down to a science. I was like, forget this, I'ma prove them wrong.

SHAR: My full name's Shahrnush.

ELLIOT: Shahrnush. That's beautiful.

SHAR: I used to get so much shit about my name. In tenth grade I saw this flier: "Shahrnush Parsipur Book Reading." Total revelation: there were other Shahrnushes in the world. She's an Iranian novelist, what she read, it was magic-realism—a woman turns into a tree so she can stay a virgin. This character plants herself in the ground, takes root in the earth and her body becomes the trunk of a tree. So the Q&A comes, someone asks about Charles Dickens, and Shahrnush says yes, she's read *Great Expectations* like forty times, including— drumroll—while in prison. Which is how I found out she had been a political prisoner in Iran, multiple times, she heard them executing people in the courtyard while she was in solitary. Still, she said, "Even in the darkness there are moments of great joy." Anyway, you're given a name, I know we have no choice in the matter, but you still have to live up to it, you have to earn your name, and I was like that is deeper than I want to live up to. So I became Shar.

ELLIOT: My pops and grandpop? Marines. My mom? Army Nurse Corps. Plus she was this like legendary community activist. You're telling me about earning a name?

ALI *(Offstage)*: Coming, my friends!

SHAR *(Looking at the plate of food)*: Shit. We're going to have to eat that.

ELLIOT: It looks like filet mignon, right?

SHAR: Dried filet with bones.

ELLIOT: Just throw it in your mouth. Don't chew, just swallow.

SHAR: There's piss draining out in the street in little rivers. It's not even covered. And we're supposed to eat straight-up off the floor.

ELLIOT: I miss Jamba Juice so fucking bad.

(They fist bump, then eat.)

SHAR: Mm.

ELLIOT: It's not bad. Seven out of ten.

ALI *(Enters)*: My friend is very happy! Perfect. He works for Al Jazeera. You will do the interview?

SHAR: Can I do it in English?

ALI: He is very good at English.

ELLIOT: As long as we have time to hit the sights. Because you know how Shar talks.

SHAR: Says the kettle.

ELLIOT: On and on.

ALI: Do not worry my friend. You see everything. Beautiful. I drive fast, you see whole country. *(To Shar)* He is at door. Very excited. Arab-American story. Arab in Hollywood, perfect.

SHAR: I'll do my best.

(Shar exits.)

ALI *(Sitting)*: You like wrestling?

ELLIOT: Eh. I used to.

ALI: My little boy has Hulk Hogan DVD.

ELLIOT: Old-school.

ALI: You like football? Soccer?

ELLIOT: I don't know shit about football except you kick the ball in the net and yell GOAL!!!

ALI: This is it! You know football!

ELLIOT: No TV, let's just talk. You think this movie's gonna be good?

ALI: Nigel is smart man. Good listener. Not idiot. Sharp like tack!

ELLIOT: It's nice living in the barracks with the guys again. I told Nigel, you want to do it right? These guys can't live in no hotel, they gotta build barracks from the ground up and stay in it. Cuz that camaraderie? You can't get that in normal life.

ALI: Every army, full of many brothers.

ELLIOT: And the adrenaline? From being in a firefight? From going house to house, not knowing if there's a bullet waiting for you on the other side of the door?

ALI: You like this adrenaline?

ELLIOT: It reminds you you're alive.

ALI: Me? Not so good with adrenaline.

ELLIOT: Did you see a lot of action? In the Jordanian army?

ALI: A lot of action. But not Jordanian army.

ELLIOT: I thought . . .

ALI: Iraqi Armed Forces.

ELLIOT: Iraqi?

ALI: Too much adrenaline. Adrenaline all the time. This is why I leave Iraq.

ELLIOT: Wait. How long you been here?

ALI: Five years.

ELLIOT: The way you talk about Jordan. I thought you were like born and raised. It's like people in Philly be talking 'bout cheesesteaks.

ALI: Do not tell guys on film crew. Maybe they treat me different. Like I take their job. Maybe they report and my family is sending back to Iraq.

ELLIOT: Does Nigel know?

ALI: Why you think he hires me? You are expert on United States Marines. I am expert on Iraqi culture. I am telling him, "Yes, Iraqi would do this. Yes, Iraqi would say this. No, wrong wrong wrong." Nigel gives me money so my daughter put in private school.

ELLIOT: How did he find you?

ALI: Craigslist. "Expert in Iraqi culture, no papers necessary, pay in cash." He receives two thousand emails for this ad.

ELLIOT: Damn.

ALI: Many of us here. In Iraq, they were doctor. University professor. Here, hiding, afraid, learning Jordan accent so nobody notice. I tell my daughter, do not talk at school, only listen, write, nod head yes, shake head no. No talking until Jordanian accent is perfect. My wife? Do you see her hands?

ELLIOT: No.

ALI: Always tremble. I buy her antidepressants, very expensive. She calls her father. "Baba, baba, help me go back to Iraq. Baba help me go home." He says, "No no no, crazy! Help me leave Iraq and come to Jordan."

ELLIOT: Yo . . . half the shit I said on set. During the actors boot camp? Things I said about Iraq, shit I did there?

ALI: Half the time, you speak from heart. Half the time, from other place.

ELLIOT: Yo man if I had known . . .

ALI: My lovely, most people speak from other place one hundred percent!

ELLIOT: Why the hell are you so nice to me? I'm already here thinking, I don't deserve this. A second chance to meet the Arab culture.

ALI: You think you had real first chance?

ELLIOT: Why would you bring me into your home?

ALI: I am like you. We are same. Xerox copy. Optimist. Always laugh laugh good time. Nice person. But inside heart, person who is different.

ELLIOT: You got anyone still there?

ALI: My mother and father.

ELLIOT: You got anyone young there?

ALI: My cousin Nasser. Very short and fat man. Always he wants to play basketball but he is short and wide like hafilah.

ELLIOT: Bus?

ALI: Good Arabic my brother. He stays in Iraq, to rebuild. Iraqi National Basketball Association. He tries to create this. Smart man.

ELLIOT: I got something. If you could send something to him. Maybe he could track down an address and deliver it?

(Elliot pulls a passport from his pocket, gives it to Ali.)

ALI: This is Iraqi passport.

(Silence.)

This is Iraqi person you know?

(Silence.)

ELLIOT: He's my first.

(Silence.)

ALI: Why you bring this today?

ELLIOT: Every day. It lives in my pocket. Every day since 2003 it's in my pocket.

(Silence.)

There's an address here, I'm guessing it's his. Maybe your cousin Nasser could go there. I know it's a big country. But if you could send it to him and maybe he could go there and give it back to the family. Give it to his wife and son.

ALI: How you know he has wife and son?

ELLIOT: After I . . . I seen them . . .

(Elliot pulls money out of his pocket, hands it to Ali.)

How much does it cost to send a package to Iraq? Or actually, to send a messenger? I want to send money so Nasser can get a driver and go to this address.

ALI: Put this money away.

ELLIOT: For you to send the package. You gotta send it secure, it has to make it there.

ALI: You pay, I take you to Petra. You pay, I take you to Dead Sea. This, you do not pay.

(Elliot puts the money back in his pocket.)

ELLIOT: My cousin's address is on the back. That can be the return address in case it doesn't work out.

ALI: You live with this cousin, Yazmin?

ELLIOT: No but I gave up my apartment to come film this movie so at the moment I have no return address.

ALI: How you know I don't put this in trash can?

(Silence. Ali puts the passport in his pocket.)

No forgive. I cannot forgive. But you know real who I am. I know real who you are. Witness for each other.

Scene 5

Skype.

ELLIOT: Yo, Petra? Yaz, I know you seen the Eiffel Tower, Greek theaters and Big Ben and shit, but *Yaz.* You take a horseback ride to a crack in the mountain. The horses drop you off at the crack, then you walk. As you come around the last turn, you see this giant building carved *into the mountain.* It's thousands of years old. Scientists have measured and the buildings are within an inch of being perfect.

YAZ *(Squinting)*: This image is weird. Your eyebrows look all white.

ELLIOT: That's the Dead Sea.

YAZ: Are you there? I said your eyebrows look weird.

ELLIOT: The Dead Sea is on my eyebrows.

YAZ: Okay.

ELLIOT: The water is thirty-percent salt. The way tourists do it, they go through a hotel, and take a shower after.

We just pulled over on the side of the road, climbed on some rocks, and started floating around in the water. I was like, "Let's go skinny-dipping!" Shar went in her tank top and thong.

YAZ: Who's Shar?

ELLIOT: One of the actors. We were just floating around with our asses in the air. So on the car ride home we started, our skin literally started crystallizing. I am white, covered in crystals. I look like Storm. My armpits look like a geode from the Natural Sciences Museum. Wanna see?

YAZ: I'm good, thanks!

(Shar enters, licks Elliot's cheek.)

SHAR: You taste like the rim of a margarita.

(Shar exits.)

YAZ: Uh . . .

ELLIOT: What?

YAZ: Ummm . . .

ELLIOT: Oh that? Girls just be randomly tasting Big El up in the Middle East.

YAZ: Oh Jesus Lord.

(Lefty enters Yaz's space.)

LEFTY: The cement is all dry, mom.

YAZ: Lefty, come say hi. You remember my cousin Elliot?

(Lefty looks at the laptop screen, waves.)

ELLIOT: Lefty is that you? Yo, Lefty! Damn, you don't change, do you?

LEFTY: Elliot's on the TV.

ELLIOT: Yup, and on the silver screen soon! You still keep traffic flowing at 7th and Venango?

LEFTY: 2nd and Erie now. A little boy died there so I direct traffic now so no more little kids die. There's a lot of teddy bears on the pole where he died.

ELLIOT: Still being traffic cop! Yo, you're the best traffic cop North Philly's ever seen!

LEFTY: Tomorrow I'm gonna go to the thrift store and get another teddy bear. Because Yaz gave me twenty dollars. I'm gonna tie another teddy bear to the pole.

ELLIOT: You do that, Lefty.

LEFTY *(To Yaz)*: What can I do next?

YAZ: Sit, relax.

LEFTY: I want a task.

YAZ: Are all the folding chairs out back?

(Lefty exits.)

ELLIOT: So . . . You like a boy?

YAZ: I gotta jet. I got twelve cases of beer at the distributor.

ELLIOT: Twelve cases?!

YAZ: My party starts in four hours! Logging off.

ELLIOT: Wait wait wait. Yaz. Did you sleep with this guy yet?

YAZ: Oh Lord Jesus.

ELLIOT: Cousin to cousin. This is a safe forum.

YAZ: No I did not sleep with the guy.

ELLIOT: Heavy petting? Over the panties?

YAZ: Forget I said anything. It's purely hypothetical, this crush which is not even a crush. It's *nothing*.

ELLIOT: Like "nothing" nothing?

YAZ: Shut up.

ELLIOT: You are in love like tostones are in grease!

YAZ: Listen. Remember how we pinky swore we'd never have kids?

ELLIOT: There's a sparkle in your eye!

YAZ: We were sitting in my room playing Super Mario. It was the week after Titi Odessa . . .

ELLIOT: There's a bluebird on your gat-damn shoulder!

YAZ: You're not listening!

ELLIOT: It was the week after she overdosed for the first time. I am listening. I'm just trying not to get sucked into your Bermuda Triangle of depressing shit.

YAZ: And we saw all those tubes running in and out of her? And we swore we'd never have kids cuz it would be like putting cracked mirrors and black cats directly into someone's DNA?

ELLIOT: It's called a condom. Look into it. Back to real shit, how's the dude's breath?

YAZ: Fumy.

ELLIOT: Before you jump into bed, give a motherfucker a Tic Tac. And Yaz, serious? Don't be wearing those granny panties you be wearing.

YAZ: How the hell do you know what panties I wear?

ELLIOT: They be sticking like a foot up above your jeans. Shit goes up to your armpits, like a turtleneck.

YAZ: I hate you!

ELLIOT: With an elastic band so thick you could use it as a trampoline.

YAZ: Good-bye!

ELLIOT: Yo your butt cheeks will thank me! After being trapped all those years, your ass will be breathing!

YAZ: Yes, real ladies only wear floss in their ass. I'm logging off!

ELLIOT: Ya ya ya en serio. *(Completely earnest)* Your under-wear is California king-size.

YAZ *(Logging off)*: Oh my god!

ELLIOT: I love you, too!

Scene 6

North Philadelphia.

The Musicians play a traditional parranda drinking song. Lights rise on North Philly. Agustín and Yaz are joyous, and drunk as skunks. Agustín's cuatro is broken in half. He cradles it lovingly. Dirty Styrofoam plates and half-filled plastic cups are piled up everywhere.

AGUSTÍN: Oooh, mamita, you're drunker than me!

YAZ: Oh my god! The next time I throw a party I don't care what holiday it is! That shit is happening in June. Fucking . . . July. I'm throwing Three Kings in the summer! It's cold as shit!

AGUSTÍN: All of North Philly came out tonight!

YAZ: I swear the house was about to collapse. When the walls started shaking that was it, I was like, all right, everyone out! Party ov-uh! Viejo, the sun's practically about to rise!

AGUSTÍN: Every time I turn around you're pulling chicken wings from the closet, lasagna from the cabinets. I'm thinking, how much food can one woman cook?

YAZ: You saw all them greedy grubbers walking off with two extra plates, "Ay for my cousin, ay for my sick Titi, ay my Chihuahua only eats spare ribs nothing else."

AGUSTÍN: Y los gringos? Those white folks dancing and singing like Pentecostals on Sunday morning. I said, mira pa'lla, they're more Puerto Rican than me!

YAZ: That's who I was telling you about. The new neighbors across from Doña Luisa! They showed up at midnight informing me they had called the cops. So what did I do? Did I get barrio on their ass? I got abuela on their ass. I served them some relleno de papas—

AGUSTÍN: Relleno de papas? I didn't get any!

YAZ: You gotta act fast, man! *(Snaps)* Ay, those gringos Loved. My. Food, Agustín! Next thing I know the Partridge Family is playing güiro and maracas while you sing "En Mi Viejo San Juan."

AGUSTÍN *(Singing)*:
> Me voy, ya me voy,
> Pero un día volveré . . .

YAZ: And when the cops showed up? Compadre, I pulled out my coquito . . .

AGUSTÍN: You still have coquito left from Christmas? Carrrrrajo! Liar!

YAZ: I put it in a Mylanta bottle so you wouldn't find it. One bottle, special reserve, for emergency use only. Those cops were at the front door talking about, "Do you have a permit? Public nuisance. Public disturbance. Let me see your hands." I said, oye, before you cuff me, try this coquito. An hour later they're packing up two plates of food for their families. And the short one? The redheaded leprechaun-looking cop? He asked me to the Flyers game this Sunday!

AGUSTÍN: Did you say yes?

YAZ: Ay muchacho, wouldn't you like to know?

(Yaz finds a little tin, offers it to Agustín.)

Tic Tac?

AGUSTÍN: Gracias.

(He takes one.)

I haven't played like that since, imagínate, since we marched on the nation's capital. You, me, Elliot, his mom singing boleros to Bill Clinton! All them whites and blacks and chinos marching at our side for the Boricua cause, telling me, "Man I ain't never heard music like that." I said, "Oye, the songs are pretty but make no mistake. Each song is a revolutionary song. Each song is a protest. A declaration of what belongs to us!"

YAZ: You know what I realized about the cuatro tonight? It's an outlet for the men. You can make a string quiver like laughter but you can also make it moan like crying. It's the one acceptable way a Puerto Rican man can cry.

AGUSTÍN: I'm holding a funeral for this beautiful instrument. The only woman I ever loved . . .

YAZ: It looks like you played baseball with this thing.

AGUSTÍN: Someone must have sat on her or stepped on her.

YAZ: I'll order you a new one from Puerto Rico. That's how I'll pay you for playing all night.

AGUSTÍN: I'm too old to start over. A new cuatro won't have the memories.

YAZ: I bet there's old ones on eBay.

AGUSTÍN: A dinosaur like me can't last much longer.

YAZ: Well. A consolation prize.

(She hands him a little gift box.)

This goes against all my feminist principles.

AGUSTÍN: For me?

YAZ: For me, technically.

(He opens it, pulls out a lacy thong.)

AGUSTÍN: Ay dios mio.

YAZ: Do you have herpes?

AGUSTÍN: Yazmin!

YAZ: We're not gonna use a condom and I ain't bringing you into my OBGYN for no test. So . . . STDs? HIV? Creepy crawlies? Speak to me of your history.

AGUSTÍN: No. Me? No, I do not. No history.

YAZ: I'm glad we had this conversation. Now I'll go put this on . . .

AGUSTÍN: No. Wait. All the lights have to be out.

YAZ: Ay, please!

AGUSTÍN: You don't want to see this old skin. I'm like a shoe that's been left in the closet too many years.

YAZ: Did you bring a sheet with a hole cut in it, too? When's the last time you . . . ?

AGUSTÍN: With someone your age? When I was your age.

YAZ: I'll go slip into this. With the lights on.

AGUSTÍN: No! Yazmin. We have to turn off the lights and even then I'll shut my eyes tight. I want to do this but in the dark.

YAZ: What are you talking about?

AGUSTÍN: I can't see you that way, it's inappropriate. You are my neighbor, the closest friend I've had in a long time.

YAZ: This sounds like a breakup speech!

AGUSTÍN: I just want to focus on the task at hand.

YAZ: Which is what? Are we coming together? Or am I providing DNA?

(*A knock at the door.*)

Lefty!

AGUSTÍN (*Cramping up*): Ay, this damn arm.

(*Another knock.*)

(*In pain*) Do you have any Tylenol?

YAZ: I don't want to turn him away if you and I are going to be sitting around all night playing bingo.

AGUSTÍN: Don't let him in.

(*Yaz opens the door, but doesn't let Lefty in.*)

YAZ: It's late, Lefty. It's three in the morning.

LEFTY: I got scared, mom.

YAZ: Why?

LEFTY: The teddy bears on the pole.

YAZ: Lefty . . .

LEFTY: Someone took the teddy bears off the pole. And the candle jars. And the fake flowers and Tweety Bird balloon and the kite shaped like a bumblebee. There was a purple jump rope, there was a Styrofoam cross. There were two little virgin statues. Now the corner is empty and no one will know a kid died there anymore.

YAZ: I told you to get to the shelter by eight.

LEFTY: I had to direct traffic, mom.

YAZ: Don't make me put you out on the street, Lefty. You have to get to the shelters in time! Do you still have the twenty I gave you?

45

LEFTY: Yes, mom.

YAZ: Let me see it.

(He shows her the twenty.)

Go to the diner on Erie. Kill time there for a few hours. Come back at sunrise and you can sleep on my couch for a little, okay? But let's not make a habit of this.

AGUSTÍN: Lefty, before you go.

(Agustín goes into his guitar case and takes out a piece of paper, shows it to Lefty.)

(Reading) "Frankford Creek." "Wingohocking Creek." "Tacony Creek." "Wissinoming Creek." "Shackaminsing Creek."

LEFTY: That's a nice map.

AGUSTÍN: All the old streams in the city.

LEFTY: It looks like the veins on the back of my hand.

AGUSTÍN: They used to be on the surface. The city was covered in them.

(He hands the map to Lefty.)

A gift from my friend at the water department.

LEFTY: Did you see, mom?

YAZ: Lefty. Come back in a few hours. I'll look at it then.

LEFTY: Yes, mom.

(He goes. She closes the door.)

YAZ: Now I'll be thinking of Lefty. Out all night in the freezing cold. How's your arm?

AGUSTÍN: It goes away like that. *(Snaps)*

YAZ: I can tell it's bothering you. There's ibuprofen in the medicine cabinet.

(He shrugs.)

Here's how you know I'm old.

AGUSTÍN: Don't say that to a man twenty years older than you.

YAZ: I don't believe in soul mates. Good night, Agustín.

AGUSTÍN: Yazmin.

YAZ: Let yourself out.

AGUSTÍN: Can I rub your foot?

YAZ: Leave the door unlocked, all right?

AGUSTÍN: I'm an old car that's been buried under the snow all winter. I just need to warm up for a minute, run the engine. Let me tell you a story.

YAZ: I've heard them all. Twice.

AGUSTÍN: Even the Celia Cruz one?

YAZ: Ay, what an exaggerator!

AGUSTÍN: Siéntate. Give me your foot.

(She doesn't.)

Yazmin. The queen of salsa signed a coconut to me!

YAZ: Bullshit.

(She sits, puts her foot out. He takes her shoe off, starts to rub her foot.)

AGUSTÍN: I did a concert in Miami with Celia. Fíjate, that was the highlight, meng! We were at this fancy bar, drinking coconut water together, and I said to her, "Celia, it would be my great honor if you would dedicate this coconut to me." And she signed her name on it.

YAZ: Where's the coconut?

AGUSTÍN: Someone must have taken it.

(Yaz takes off her shirt. He sees her body.)

YAZ: Tell me another one.

AGUSTÍN: Back then the songs were the newspaper. The songs were what happened that day. "The Phillies won!" That would be a song. "The sugar factory is hiring!" That would be a song. Back then the songs were our literature, meng. We'd say, tomorrow, Chuy's house or Nelson's house, eight o'clock, roundtable, come ready to improvise. Then you arrive, everyone pulls out their instruments, and the host announces it. He says, here's the theme: Don Quixote. Here's the theme: President Kennedy. Here's the theme: Romeo y Julieta.

(She begins to unbutton his shirt.)

And you have to improvise a décima right there on the spot, meng! Today we have virtuosos but we don't have players. Immaculate technique but as Ramito, the voice of the mountains, used to say: menos es más. Say the most with the least.

(She takes off his shirt. She sees his body.)

YAZ: Tell me a story on the cuatro.

AGUSTÍN: It's broken.

YAZ: Then improvise, viejo.

AGUSTÍN: Bueno, imagine you are a string on the cuatro.

(Lights fade on the scene and rise on the Musicians, who play a romantic bolero.)

SCENE 7

The Film Set of *Haditha on Fire*. Azraq, Jordan.

An (unseen) dead body is on the ground. Shar leans over the body.

SHAR: Laaaaa! LAAAAA!

> *(Elliot enters, with his gun pointed at her. He is filthy, covered in blood.)*

ELLIOT: Ey, move away from the body!
SHAR *(To the body)*: Ahmad! Ahmad . . . Ahmad . . .

> *(Elliot lowers his gun.)*

ELLIOT: Come on. Move away. Come on.

> *(Shar stands, stumbles to Elliot, spits in his face. He takes it, unflinching. She tries to grab the gun from his hand*

and in an attempt to push her away, he knocks her to the ground. She returns to the body.)

SHAR: Ahmad . . . Ahmad . . . Laaaa . . . Laaaa . . .
ALI *(Half off, reading a text)*: "Cut."

(Elliot reaches for his eye.)

ELLIOT: Jesus, Shar, what did you eat for lunch, hot peppers? Get me an eye wash!
SHAR: Sorry! I aimed for your nose.
ELLIOT: You got my eyeball.

(Ali gives him a paper cup and water. Elliot rinses his eye.)

I'm good. I'm good.
SHAR *(Lying)*: You look real good, Elliot.
ELLIOT: Aimed for my nose. Yeah right.
SHAR *(Lying)*: You look like a million bucks.
ELLIOT: Just please tell me he got what he needs.
ALI: Hold on. He is texting me. *(Reads the text)* "Do it again."
ELLIOT: That motherfucker.
ALI *(Reading)*: "You sound like a dying goat. What the fuck is that?"
SHAR: I think that was to me.
ELLIOT *(Yelling out)*: Yo, Nigel, quit texting and get your fucking shot! Come on let's just do this.
SHAR: Relax. Zero stunts, in the shade.
ELLIOT: Get in your place. *(Calling out)* Ready? Roll the sound. I'm calling it! Action! *(To Shar)* Just go, I ain't waiting for him no more. *(Calling out)* ACTION!

(Shar gets in place, just like at the top of the scene.)

SHAR: Laaaaa! LAAAAA!

(Elliot enters, with his gun pointed at her. He is filthy, covered in blood.)

ELLIOT: Ey, move away from the body!
SHAR *(To the body)*: Ahmad! Ahmad . . . Ahmad . . .

(Elliot lowers his gun.)

ELLIOT: Come on. Move away. Come on.

(Shar stands, stumbles to Elliot, spits in his face. He takes it, unflinching. She tries to grab his gun, and in an attempt to push her away, he knocks her to the ground, more violently this time. He stands above her, presses his rifle into her face, clearly going off-script.)

I said get the fuck away from the body! You think I'm playing with you?!
ALI: Cut!

(Elliot doesn't move, but Shar hurries away from him.)

SHAR: I got your nose that time! Elliot! Elliot!
ALI *(Enters with cup)*: Eye bath?

(Elliot is almost statue still, except that he's crying. You can just barely tell.)

SHAR: Elliot?

(Ali's phone beeps.)

ALI: This is Nigel. *(Reading)* "That's a wrap."
SHAR: See Elliot, scene's done.

(Ali's phone beeps again.)

ALI *(Reading)*: "Actors must pack clothes. Meet at van in forty-five minutes."
SHAR: What?

(Ali's phone beeps again.)

ALI: Nigel.

(And again.)

Nigel.

(And again.)

Nigel.

(Ali's phone rings. He answers.)

My director, everything is okay?

(Ali listens.
In a separate space: lights rise in Philadelphia. Yaz stares at her ringing cell phone. She doesn't recognize the number.)

YAZ: Hello? *(Listens)* Hi, Miriam . . . Is something wrong? Yes, I'm sitting down. *(Upset)* When?
ALI *(Into the phone)*: But Egypt is two countries away from Jordan. *(Listens)* But protest is mostly not violent. Peaceful demonstration.

(He hangs up.)

Studio is worrying about Egypt. Insurance is worrying. Actors must go to hotel in Amman.

SHAR: What hotel? When?

ALI: Immediately. Four-star hotel, good security. If Mubarak is resigning, probably celebration, back to Jerash, keep filming movie. If Mubarak is not resigning, studio thinks violence, actors fly to L.A., movie is delayed.

SHAR: Delayed?! Jesus. Elliot, did you hear that? Elliot?

(Elliot will not move. If he moves, he will cry. And everyone will see him. So he stands completely still.)

YAZ *(Emotional, into the phone)*: He was just here Friday night at my parranda, singing, playing . . . If there's anything I can do, Miriam . . . How can I help?

SHAR: Elliot . . .

(Shar takes Elliot's hand. Now he must stand even more still or he'll weep like a child.)

ALI: My brother.

(Ali takes his other hand. It passes, like an electric current, through them. They will all weep if they move. So they stand still.)

My brother, it was a beautiful scene.

(Intermission.)

Prologue

A traditional song warned Puerto Ricans living in the U.S. that we don't have the virtue of conserving our youth, that we will continue growing old until our feet forget the path back to those soft-sand beaches. I used to think it was being here that made those distant mountains glow so green, that only a remembered sunrise could be that golden. Until we visit, and I remember, all over again, that nostalgia is not a lie but a force that clings us to the yesterday we owe a great debt to.

In the performance space the Musicians walk us back to the debts we carry in our history.

Act Two

Center City, Philadelphia.

A press conference. Yaz is in a suit.

YAZ: Thank you. Miriam Moreno, Agustín's widow, asked me to speak on behalf of the family so they can grieve in privacy. At approximately 4:30 A.M. yesterday Agustín Moreno checked into the Kappa Health Partners emergency room complaining of pain in his left arm. He was told to have a seat and suffered a heart attack within ten minutes of sitting down. For the next hour he sat dead, slumped over in his chair, in full view of the security guard and reception desk. No one lifted a finger. He was finally discovered dead because he was being robbed of his wristwatch and was not resisting. The mayor's office and the district attorney will speak after me and I trust it will not be canned, I trust it will not be, "We take this very seriously, etc., and so on." It is time to acknowl-

57

edge, in plain detail, the understaffed hospitals, the occupational callousness, the decisions based on ethnic and economic bias, and how no one should ever die like this in the United States of America. Agustín Moreno was a high school guidance counselor, six months short of retiring with pension, and he had health insurance. Kappa Health Partners has no statement at this time? I have prepared a statement for them. This is their *second* preventable emergency-room death this year they took more than half an hour to notice. They have three inpatient deaths currently under investigation including a grandmother who drowned because her tracheotomy had not been cleaned in days.

I can only pray, dear God, that maybe one person is watching, maybe two people are seeing this today, who will continue Agustín's work in the community. Here is what you have to do:

Take your music to people who don't know anything about Puerto Rico or North Philadelphia, and teach.

Take it to 5th and Lehigh and create a festival of Bomba y Plena.

Take your music to City Hall and take it to Doña Rita's sick bed.

Then grab ahold of a güiro player and go out to the maximum security prison at Graterford and bring tears of memory and joy to men who made a mistake or are paying for someone else's mistake.

And next time some brass hats decide to play war games on the land of your patria, grab your guitar and jump on the next bus to Lafayette Park by the White House.

And since you will almost always be performing for free, get a job where you can help the young people of our community grow in strength and wisdom.

Then, as a new week starts, stand over by a piano and sing life into your congregation.

And don't forget, after all that, to let us know that you enjoy what you're doing.

My Philadelphia neighbors, we are calling for an immediate boycott of every Kappa Health Partners clinic in the city. Saturday morning outside the Kappa Health emergency room on Olney: it's protest time. Rain or shine, bring your signs. Bring your guitars. Bring your lozenges because we will be heard. What will we have? *Survival.* When will we demand it? Saturday. See you there.

Scene 9

A Four-Star Hotel. Amman, Jordan. February 11, 2011.

A ridiculous suite. Elliot checks out the mini fridge, the wet bar. Ali flips through channels on the TV. Shar is offstage in the bathroom.

SHAR *(Offstage)*: OH SHIT!!! Jacuzzi?! This is an Olympic pool!

ALI: Everyone else four actors in one small room. Elliot gets two-bedroom suite!

ELLIOT: A cheeseburger smile goes a long way. Beer? Coca-Cola?

ALI: My wife is texting me. "Bring home milk."

ELLIOT: "You are my brother or not my brother?" Come on, five minutes.

SHAR *(Offstage)*: Body lotion?! Hair conditioner?! AHHHHH!!!

(Elliot brings Ali a Coke, sees the TV.)

ELLIOT: Uh-oh! Someone's doing a little shopping . . .

ALI: I do not know how to find regular channel.

ELLIOT: The purchase button's right here. "Hello Titty." "Anal Avatar." 3-D.

ALI: You are true man of cinema.

ELLIOT: And you, of literature. I seen you with a magazine in one hand, and in the other hand?

ALI: In the other hand, big middle finger to my brother.

ELLIOT: Give me that.

(Elliot takes the remote, changes the channel.)

There you go. Al Jazeera.

ALI: Thank you my friend. Tahrir Square.

(They look at the TV.)

ELLIOT: Yo they put Egyptian flags on their windshield wipers? I'ma try that at the next Puerto Rican Day parade.

ALI: A sea of people.

ELLIOT: Damn. That's like the Atlantic Ocean of humans.

ALI: "Good-bye Mubarak?"

ELLIOT: "Hosni Mubarak resigns?"

ALI *(Realizing)*: We are downstairs in lobby and this is happening? I do not believe!

(Ali turns the volume extremely high: deafening crowd roars, cars honking in celebration, women shrieking joyously, songs, hands clapping, chants of celebration.
Shar enters in a hotel bathrobe.)

SHAR: Smell these bath salts, your life is literally about to change!

ELLIOT *(Pointing her to the TV)*: Dude.

ALI: Vice president. Twenty minutes ago he gives the speech.

SHAR: "The people have brought down the regime." Mubarak stepped down . . .

(They are all frozen, watching the TV.)

ELLIOT: "Hurry up?"

ALI: "Hurriya." Freedom.

(The image on the TV changes.)

SHAR: Her tears are glowing like shooting stars.

ALI: This is not "say cheese." This is *smile*. Real happiness smile.

(The image on the TV changes.)

ELLIOT: Translate, translate!

SHAR: Uh . . . she's saying, "Someone gave me this megaphone . . . because all the other protestors have lost their voice . . . so I am here to tell the whole world what Egyptians need now is—"

(Shar and Ali laugh.)

ELLIOT: What Egyptians need now is . . .

SHAR: "—lozenges."

ELLIOT: What's he saying?

ALI: "Now I taste freedom. If military takes freedom, then I know what I lose. Very happy, very scared."

ELLIOT: What's that sign say?

ALI: "Today I am a man."

ELLIOT: That one?

SHAR: "You are Egyptian, lift your head."

(The image on the TV changes again. They gasp.)

ELLIOT: That's . . .

SHAR: Wow.

ALI: Beautiful.

ELLIOT: Yo the guy who interviewed you for Al Jazeera, wasn't he about to go cover Egypt?

SHAR: Can you imagine? Which dot do you think he is?

ELLIOT: You didn't get his number by any chance?

ALI: I have.

ELLIOT: Text him: what's the best route out of Jordan?

ALI: To where?

ELLIOT: To the aorta. To Liberation Square.

ALI: In Egypt?

ELLIOT: See if he answers.

ALI: Elliot.

ELLIOT: Type.

(Ali skeptically types into his phone.)

Do our phones get wireless here?

SHAR: Mine does.

ELLIOT: Google this. Amman Jordan to Cairo Egypt directions. Actually, see if you can Google-map it. Seriously, put it in traffic mode and see how long they say.

(Shar skeptically types into her phone.)

Ali, how long a drive you think it is roughly?

ALI: Six hours, eight hours?

ELLIOT: That's nothing, blink of an eye!

ALI: Okay, have fun, I am bringing home milk for my wife.

ELLIOT: I'll pay for the gallon of milk and drop it at your house on the way.

ALI: You are batshit out of your mind.

ELLIOT: I'm serious.

SHAR: He's not serious.

ELLIOT: You're the one friending them. You're the online revolutionary. But not in the flesh, huh?

SHAR (*Reading from her phone*): There's a bus all the way south to Aqaba then a ferry then another bus to Cairo.

ELLIOT: Shar, we got four wheels in the flesh right here.

ALI: You are mentally ill patient. Very long drive.

ELLIOT: Psh, I drive from L.A. to Vegas cuz I'm bored. I drive from L.A. to Vegas for all-you-can-eat king crab legs.

ALI: That is same country. I do not know, do you have visa? How is the border right now? Do they let in Americans? Israeli border, wow, very difficult! What can we do, jump over Israel like puddle?

SHAR: Elliot, this bus-ferry thing is recommended on Trip-Advisor. Sold out today and tomorrow, soonest you can get there is Monday.

ELLIOT: No, they'll probably have us back on set Monday. *Today*. Egypt invented pyramids, they made algebra, and now they took down a dictator with Sharpie pens and Twitter. I wanna be the only Puerto Rican up in there. Ali, tolls, border fees and bribes on me, bro.

ALI: I cannot leave Jordan, I have no papers.

ELLIOT: Shit.

ALI: I thought you come up here for boom-boom together.

SHAR: Boom-boom?

ELLIOT: His words, not mine.

ALI: No, Elliot says this!

SHAR: I came for the Jacuzzi. What did you invite me here for?

ALI: Look. Boom-boom. Perfect. Good plan, stick with plan. You two, beautiful couple.

SHAR: Couple? This is getting good.

ELLIOT: Yo aren't there animals who scientifically don't need a partner? They can like do it and get pregnant all by themselves?

SHAR: Komodo dragons, banana slugs.

ELLIOT: Juilliard here is so smart she don't need a partner.

ALI: Ay. Even fighting like couple. Look. Enjoy Egyptian cotton on the bed. Enjoy boom-boom, enjoy no boom-boom. Enjoy revolution on TV.

(Ali's phone beeps.)

Reporter from Al Jazeera.

(Elliot stands with anticipation.)

"Cairo airport is open. Many journalists photographers arriving. Good luck."

ELLIOT: Shar, look up the next few flights out of Amman.

SHAR: It doesn't look like Facebook there. It looks like actual faces, eyes that look back at you.

ELLIOT: So we should eat Jiffy Pop and watch *Arab's Got Talent* all night?

SHAR: They've been dragging people through the streets.

ELLIOT: They're chanting "simliya simliya." Peaceful.

ALI *(Correcting him)*: Silmiya.

SHAR: Anderson Cooper got his ass kicked out there.

ELLIOT: By the protestors?

SHAR: By Mubarak's thugs.

ELLIOT: Who are out of a job now.

SHAR *(To Ali)*: He thinks it's cute to stick his wet finger into a socket.

ELLIOT: Whoa whoa whoa, how'd my finger get wet?

SHAR: Ten forty-five P.M. Three thirty A.M. Six A.M. There's plenty of flights, have your pick.

ELLIOT: Should we try for the 10:45?

SHAR: We?

ELLIOT: Dude, earn your name.

SHAR: People died there, those protestors haven't slept, they've prayed as bullets flew, they held hands to protect each other's prayers, they shouted things their parents were terrified to whisper. I don't get to waltz in and claim that.

ELLIOT (*To Ali*): You know what she told me when we was sitting on your living room floor?

SHAR: Elliot.

ELLIOT: That she thinks she's nothing.

SHAR: Hey.

ELLIOT: You're a quarter Egyptian.

SHAR: Don't tell me what I am.

ELLIOT: Someone needs to.

SHAR: Wow.

ELLIOT: You know what happened the first time my plane touched down in PR? How quick that shit rearranged my DNA?

SHAR: My point was it's shitty to always have to be something, to have no choice.

ELLIOT: You do have a choice, and you choose to be nothing.

SHAR: Fuck off and do not lecture me! I will be pragmatic, I will self-preserve, and I will not apologize for it, especially not to you.

ELLIOT: Okay, I'll go alone.

SHAR: Good, bon voyage.

ELLIOT (*To Shar*): Can I use your phone to buy the ticket? (*To Ali*) Give me a ride to the airport?

SHAR: He's not your staff. This isn't *Driving Miss Daisy*.

ALI: What is *Driving Miss Daisy*?

ELLIOT: An old black-and-white movie.

SHAR: Actually a play.

ALI *(To Shar)*: I do not know *Miss Daisy*. I know *Three Musketeers*. Maybe protect each other. Special day, history, opportunity. Maybe two musketeers.

ELLIOT: You said you were cracking open the book of your life. Don't you wanna see the title page?

SHAR: Doesn't anything scare you?

ELLIOT: You want to read that first sentence? Together?

(She hands him her phone.)

SHAR: See if there's two tickets for the 10:45. Business class.

ELLIOT: Let's go to Egypt! But ain't no way in hell I'm paying for no business class.

SHAR: If anything happens to me, my father will slowly and meticulously dismember you, beginning with your fingernails—

ELLIOT: Three musketeers, man. All three of us should be on that plane.

ALI: You do me favor. If you arrive in Tahrir Square, take handful of dirt, put in pocket, bring back for me. Souvenir.

ELLIOT: Deal.

Scene 10

Yaz's House. North Philadelphia.

Yaz watches her computer screen intently, looks at her watch. Lefty enters from the garden holding a large potted plant.

YAZ: Nine minutes twenty seconds. He goes in, fills out a form, sits in a chair in the corner, makes two phone calls. Nine minutes later, he just slumps over a little.

LEFTY: This is the last one, mom.

YAZ: Hm?

LEFTY: The last plant. Don't think any more will fit.

YAZ: Is it frozen?

LEFTY: As a popsicle.

YAZ: Put it in the tub. Poor things, sitting out in the freezing cold all week. I'll run a hot shower later.

LEFTY: The bathtub's full.

YAZ: I don't know, Lefty, put it on the floor! I'm trying to watch this.

LEFTY: I thought you already did.

YAZ: Agustín has a smile on his face.

LEFTY: Everyone in Heaven has a smile on their face.

YAZ: This isn't Heaven. It's the emergency room. They posted the security tapes on YouTube. People across the world can watch Agustín die.

LEFTY: No thank you, mom.

YAZ: There they go, two men taking the watch right off his wrist.

LEFTY: Stop watching that please.

YAZ: Yeah, that's a smile on his face. Just like he said it would be.

LEFTY: YOU NEED A TASK, MOM.

(Lefty moves the laptop away from Yaz. A moment.)

YAZ: I gotta print out fliers for the protest. Give me your sweatshirt, I'll go run a load of laundry. What did you do with the new clothes I bought you? That sweatshirt is from a year ago.

(Lefty shrugs, takes off his sweatshirt.)

Since when do you wear a watch?

LEFTY: Do you like it? I just got it.

YAZ: Where did you get it?

LEFTY: I don't know, mom. From . . . I think. I found it.

YAZ: Found it where?

LEFTY: The park.

YAZ: What park?

LEFTY: Norris Square?

YAZ: Are you asking me or telling me?

LEFTY: I don't remember what park.

YAZ: Lefty, start remembering.

LEFTY: I found it at the shelter.

YAZ: The one on Poplar? The one on Diamond?

LEFTY: I don't know.

YAZ: Are you lying to me?

LEFTY: No, mom.

YAZ: Then where the fuck did you get it?

LEFTY: Please don't yell at me, mom.

YAZ: Can I see? *(He doesn't show it)* It looks like Agustín's watch.

LEFTY: It's mine, fair and square.

YAZ: Since when? When did you get it?

LEFTY: You're going to be mad at me.

YAZ: Look at me Lefty! Were you in that hellhole of an emergency room?

LEFTY: No, mom, I don't think I was. I'm sure I wasn't.

YAZ: Did someone give you the watch?

LEFTY: Yes.

YAZ: Who was it, Lefty? Because I'm going to go kill that sick human being! I SAID LOOK AT ME! This is the United States of America and this is how they let their neighbor die! This is how they let a decent human being die! They took the watch off a dying man's wrist?!

LEFTY: I was at 5th and Lehigh!

YAZ: When?

LEFTY: I don't know.

YAZ: Last year? This week? WHEN? WHAT WERE YOU DOING?

LEFTY: Selling.

YAZ: Selling what?

LEFTY: I don't remember.

YAZ: LIAR. YOU TELL ME WHAT THE FUCK YOU WERE SELLING!

LEFTY: The food you gave me, mom. The ribs. I don't have no refrigerator and I was full. The man didn't have no money. No money. Just looked like a skeleton. An angry skeleton. He gave me the watch. He ate the ribs real fast.

YAZ: Go, Lefty.

LEFTY: No, mom.

YAZ: Leave. Please.

LEFTY: No, mom!

YAZ: GET OUT OF MY HOUSE!

(Lefty takes off the watch, gives it to Yaz, and exits. Yaz looks at the watch.)

It's not Agustín's watch. Lefty? Lefty!

(After a moment, Agustín enters behind her.)

What did it feel like, sitting there in that waiting room? Were you in pain? Were you scared? Did you finally realize you love me?

AGUSTÍN: Like a friend.

YAZ: Can't you lie to me in Heaven? Just lie to me a little: What was the last thing to go through your head?

AGUSTÍN: Hearing Ramito live.

YAZ: Ay, Agustín, wrong lie!

AGUSTÍN: I was stuck in Puerto Rico after a canceled flight. Hurricanes. The entire island was blowing like a hair dryer on high. The airport was chaos. A man can only beg US Air so many times. So I borrow my cousin's neighbor's Volkswagen Rabbit—poor machine can barely fart up a ten-degree incline, but I decide to drive the entire Ruta Panorámica on those four wheels. Pueblito after pueblito strung together like green Christmas lights. Palm trees, bamboo. I haven't seen a house for forty minutes, I hang a hairpin and boom: there's a little hut sticking out the side of the mountain.

Like a loose tooth poking into the sky. It looked like a gust of wind might just take it away. Black smoke puffing out from the back.

YAZ: Pig roast?

AGUSTÍN: I'm thinking, lunchtime, lechón time! I park, pebbles tumble off the cliff. I look down and see what's holding this casita up—two wooden posts stuck in the cliffside. So rotten, so crumbly, they'd snap if a pelican landed. The sign above the door says THE PHILADELPHIA INN. Carrrrajo. I go in. Dark place. How much for a Corona? No Corona. How about a Heineken? No Heineken. Bartender points to the drinks menu: Medalla in plastic cups, one quarter. Hurricane's picking up outside. Floor swaying like a fishing boat. Wind screaming and what do I hear? My anthem. The first Ramito song I ever laid ears on. A bolero dedicated to the the bull that plowed his farm for so many years, the bull he loved, who died. I say to the bartender, "I have searched every record store in Puerto Rico, in Philadelphia, in the New York subway system, I have sang this song to every radio deejay and cuatro player I know, and I tell you for a fact, this song was never recorded!" I say, "Por favor, do a man a favor and sell me this record." Bartender says, "This ain't no record," and points a fat finger to a dark corner of the shack, and my eyes adjust to make out a face. Maso Rivera, plucking away at his cuatro. Maso Rivera. The Ben Franklin of the cuatro, he put lightning into those ten strings. And behind him? Ramito himself. The master. The voice that uses nostalgia like a gat-damn machine gun. Singing my bull song. I run to my car, pull the güiro from the glove compartment, and all night: boleros, aguinaldos, seis chorreaos.

(The Musicians play a joyous cuatro song.)

People pouring into the inn, shouting requests, tapping their wedding rings on the counter in rhythm. "Wepa! All the beers are on me!" I'm seasick from the floor, swooping, swaying. I say, "Oye, Ramito, your voice has reached new levels of sadness. How do you cry like that when singing?" He said, "They tell me the cancer is everywhere. In my earlobes, in my pinky, a few tumors right on my vocal cords." Then he tells me, "I was up all night holding a gun between my teeth." I said, "Ramito, no offense, don't take this the wrong way, but you're dead, aren't you?" He gives me a glance like, "Ey, what can you do?" I said, "Maso Rivera, if memory serves, you died a while back didn't you?" "2001," he tells me. And the next set begins. Every Medalla beer I'm getting lighter and lighter. I'm sprouting wings, 'cept instead of feathers it's beer cans, which is how I got here, mija. Surfing a hurricane, flying while intoxicated, to tell you this: never let those strings lie still.

YAZ: What strings, your broken cuatro?

AGUSTÍN: There's a guy in Boston who does great repairs. There's a cuatro maker in Barranquitas, he fixes them up like new. Mamita, do it yourself, get some Gorilla Glue. But if she is not played? Broken pottery and arrowheads will bubble to the surface. Indian skulls and slave spines and finger bones that signed the Declaration of Independencia. Philly will float out to sea if those strings lie still. Yazmin, amor de mi vida, love of my life, bring her to me. Let me show you how the jigsaw pieces fit together.

(Yazmin goes into a closet, grabs the broken cuatro, goes to hand it to Agustín, but he's already gone. As lights fade on Yaz, they rise on the Musicians, who sing a few joyous verses over the riffs they've been playing all along.)

SCENE 11

Skype.

ELLIOT: Twenty minutes outside of Cairo, traffic came to a standstill. There was a billboard of Mubarak ten meters off the ground. People were on the pavement, on their hands and knees making a human ladder.

YAZ: Why?

ELLIOT: So that someone could literally climb up on their backs and rip Mubarak's face down. It was two college-looking kids. They climbed up real careful.

YAZ: You saw this?

ELLIOT: Barely, it was dark out but we hopped out the cab and joined in. I could feel the sneaker in my back. Everyone was just calm, just breathing together. Then you could hear the paper of the billboard start to rip. Everyone wanted to cheer, but you can't or else we'll fall down and crush each other. So people were just breathing without cheering, Yazmin, electric. All you

could see was brooms, people sweeping the street, clear-
ing concertina wire in the dark. We swept up pieces
of Mubarak's face like you sweep ginkgo leaves off a
stoop. I forgot for a second, I almost texted a picture to
Agustín. Thinking about all them rallies he would drag
us to. He was a monster of the Puerto Rican protest.

YAZ: They reopened the hospital.

ELLIOT: That fast, huh?

YAZ: Guess how many people showed up to *my* protest?

ELLIOT: I don't know.

YAZ: Eleven. There were flyers in every church. *Al Día* published the details online and in print. Spanish radio
announced it. Consilio and Aspira did e-blasts. Everyone
I cook for said they would be there. But it drizzled, two
drops of water, not enough to put a kink in my hair—
When the cops saw how few people came they actually
laughed, they just drove away. When the Action News
van pulled up? They were like, "Where's the protest?"
I had to lie, "Oh it already happened, it was a really quick
one." Even the reporter was trying to make me feel better, "Oh, there's a big vote in city hall today. The soda tax
vote. Even if the protest was huge it probably wouldn't
make the news." I'm like, "Thank you for rubbing that
salt really damn deep." People waltz up my steps, let
themselves in, sit at my table, they don't even ask, they
just wait to be served, not to mention all them "friends"
Agustín ever gave a free music lesson to. I could've
stayed in Center City instead of this shit, I could be
with my central air and doorman and skyline view, but
I came to this neighborhood and opened my door and
asked them to give ten minutes out of their day. They
can all feed their own damn kids now, people can go
cook their own dinner. Yazmin's kitchen is closed. Private property. Keep out of my garden. No trespassing—

ELLIOT: Dude. Cancel class. Grab a vampire book. Drive to the Jersey Shore. Eat a funnel cake.

YAZ: The boy I had a crush on, it was Agustín.

ELLIOT: Conyo . . . Pero, Yazmin, why you like them old heads? I know wine gets better with time, but men?

YAZ: It's not funny. You never let me be sad!

ELLIOT: The first music lesson he gave me, I had to pluck one string over and over. Thirty minutes of that and then I had to practice that one note the entire week. I was like, Teach me a song, bro. He was like, "menos es más, say the most with the least."

YAZ: There's an unopened box of pregnancy tests in my bathroom.

ELLIOT: Shit.

YAZ: It's too early to tell. I know you're out there making us proud but when you get a minute, come home?

ELLIOT: Yeah it may take me a minute but I'll be there.

(Ali enters.)

ALI: Finally. All morning I am calling you.

ELLIOT: My phone died on the plane. We just rolled in. You good?

ALI: My brother . . .

ELLIOT: Yaz, two minutes, do not log off.

YAZ: I'm out, I gotta go lock my front door.

(She logs off unceremoniously.)

ELLIOT: What's going on?

ALI: I am asking favor. I will not come to work for two days, three days.

ELLIOT: What happened?

ALI: Hiding for a little bit. Maybe a week.

ELLIOT: Ali . . .

ALI: My wife takes daughter to school this morning, there is headmaster standing, waiting, not friendly, asking her, "Where you are from? Let me see papers. Are you citizen?"

ELLIOT: I mean, can they do anything to you?

ALI: Yes, they can deport. Many people they send back to Iraq. I think maybe move apartment, maybe hiding for a little. Daughter does not go to school for a little. Change phone number. Temporary. Precaution.

ELLIOT: Where you gonna go?

ALI: To a family friend, someone I help, also from Iraq. One-bedroom apartment but if many families need to share—

ELLIOT: You need some money?

ALI: Do me favor. Tell Nigel I am sick. If he does not know, better. Maybe Nigel hires new Iraqi expert. Here. Phone number of university professor who knows good detail, real Iraqi. Movie should be accurate.

ELLIOT: Fuck the movie. That's the last thing on my mind right now.

ALI: Elliot, don't be crazy. Always you are crazy.

(Ali gets a text.)

"Where the fuck is my lead actor?" Time for wardrobe.

ELLIOT: Ali.

(Ali hands Elliot the cell phone.)

ALI: Here, give phone back to Nigel.

ELLIOT: How do I get in touch with you?

ALI: I call you in two days, no problem.

ELLIOT: Two days, give me your word.

ALI: Two weeks, maximum. Not worry, I do not forget passport agreement.

ELLIOT: You got too much on your plate.

ALI: No no no, already I send passport to my cousin, Nasser.

ELLIOT: I didn't forget my promise either.

(Elliot pulls a plastic baggie out of his pocket. It is full of dirt. He gives it to Ali.)

ALI: Good-luck charm. Egypt freedom dirt.

ELLIOT: Revolution in a bag, bro.

ALI: Thank you, my lovely.

SCENE 12

North Philadelphia. Twelve Months Later.

Yaz's house, late at night, the lights are out. There is knocking at the door.

YAZ: Lefty? Lefty is that you? Ya voy! Ay thank god.

(*More knocking.*)

I'm coming! Hold your horses. Lefty? Did you finally come back?

ELLIOT (*Offstage*): Yo! I need a midnight munchie! I want me some bistec encebollado!

YAZ (*Recognizing the voice*): Motherfucker. (*Letting him in*) I don't get to pinch that cheek for a whole year. Twelve months straight! I'm stuck following your Facebook page like one of those thirty thousand "friends" you have?

ELLIOT: A lot of people love me, baby.

YAZ: Don't talk to me. You were supposed to come home straight after filming. My little cheeseburger smile traveling the world, doing film festivals all around the great green globe. I'm mad at you, give me that cheek!

ELLIOT: Who never picks up her phone?

YAZ: I know, I'm sorry.

ELLIOT: "Straight to Voice Mail" should be your middle name. You good?

YAZ: I wake up, go teach, order Chinese for dinner, go to sleep.

ELLIOT: It's been a year since he died. Time to let go, dude.

YAZ: You owe me stories, a lot of them.

ELLIOT: Give me a snack, I'll start talking.

YAZ: Where have you been?

ELLIOT: In a far-off land called love . . .

YAZ: When do I get to meet this mysterious Shar?

ELLIOT: Got enough ingredients for an extra guest?

YAZ: Open door, open stove.

ELLIOT: Your door was locked. *(Going to the door)* Come in, Shar. Careful, the railing's loose. Watch that step.

SHAR *(Offstage)*: I know how to walk, Elliot.

(Shar enters. She is visibly pregnant.)

Hi. I'm Shahrnush.

YAZ: Hi. I'm Yazmin. Elliot?

ELLIOT: Will you be the godmother?

YAZ: Will I be the godmother?

SHAR: Will you be the godmother?

YAZ: Will I be the godmother? Sit! Eat! Drink! Oh my god. *(Noticing a ring)* Wait. No. Wait! Oh my god, don't tell me you went to frickin' Elvis's chapel to make it legit? Elliot!

ELLIOT: We tried to do it in Dubai, but it's like crazy regulations, paperwork. So we hopped a plane to Cyprus and it was like, "Do you? Do you? Yes. Yes."

YAZ: Welcome to the family. You look different without the thing, without the veil. You were outstanding. The death scene? Whew, that was rough.

ELLIOT: You saw the movie?

YAZ: No thanks to you. I drove to New York to see it. Sit, sit! Oh my god, you're one of those jaw-dropping halo-of-light pregnant women. You are lit from within. You're stunning. You're far too good for Elliot, I can tell already.

SHAR: I completely agree. What have I got myself into?

ELLIOT: Once my hook catches you, you can't resist. I'm magnetic.

YAZ: Excuse me. You're grounded. You're in big trouble. Berlin Film Festival? Dubai Film Festival?

(Yaz brings them snacks and drinks as he talks.)

ELLIOT: Yo, Dubai was crazy. They bought us a first-class ticket. The rooms were a thousand a night. I had a twenty-four-hour butler tuck me in.

SHAR: Dubai's so perfect it's fake. Even the palm trees were put there.

ELLIOT: I would sneeze, by the time I lifted my head, there's three people with tissues. I say, "I'm thirsty," like six sampler glasses of juice just appear. At the opening-night party, the Crown Prince of Dubai was there. All of his security was standing next to me. I got a three-foot hookah in my arm, I'm blowing smoke in his face, I'm drunk as hell, stumbling. We're in the hotel lobby balling, doing pimp shit, smoking Cuban cigars, and he's high-fiving me!

YAZ *(To Shar)*: You know how to pick 'em.

SHAR: I'm no angel.

ELLIOT: Who do you think got me the hookah? Who do you think gave me the araq?

YAZ: Araq?

ELLIOT: This liquor that's thick as hell. Like absinthe.

SHAR: Stuff you don't drink for fun. Stuff you drink to kill yourself.

ELLIOT: Like you don't say to a friend, "Let's go out and grab some araq!" No. The morning after the red carpet? Nigel, the director, calls me, eight A.M. I was so hungover, it felt like someone was kicking me in the face. "Elliot, good news, you were runner-up for best actor." I was like, "Yeah?" I'm screaming, like, "Ahhhh!" He's like, "Elliot, you didn't win." I was like, "Ahhhh!" "No no no, Elliot, you did not win." I was like, "I ain't care, I'm runner-up! Ahhh!"

YAZ: Well, I see you learned some humility in your travels abroad. You really learned a lot about culture.

SHAR: He's a bear. He talks up the high life. But even in a bad circumstance . . . He's a goofball who cries in his sleep.

ELLIOT: No I don't.

SHAR: Sometimes loud, sometimes just whimpers.

YAZ: Are you having nightmares again?

ELLIOT: Don't listen to her.

SHAR: I recorded it on my phone a few times and played it for him in the morning. It really freaked me out at first.

YAZ: We'll talk.

ELLIOT: Change the subject!

YAZ: Hey, you got a package from Jordan. It's been sitting in my cabinet forever.

(Yaz finds a padded envelope, hands it to Elliot.)

ELLIOT: When did you get this?

YAZ: Months back. I thought I told you.

ELLIOT: You didn't tell me.

YAZ: It's been that kind of year, my mind's all over the place.

(Elliot opens it, pulls out a handwritten note. Ali appears, separately.)

ALI: My brother Elliot,

I am sorry we do not see each other again, but I keep my promise. I send passport to my basketball cousin in Baghdad. He goes to Tikrit, finds the address. Woman comes to the door in pink hijab. Very nice, chit-chat, chubby woman who likes to talk. She gives my cousin tea. He decides, not going to show passport. He pretends, he is saying, "Husband is at work today?" She says American soldier shoots him in face. He is pretending surprise. American soldier spits on body, she says. American soldier takes wallet and runs away. Her son is seeing this. Four years old. Little boy always talking talking big storytelling, he does not talk after this. Eight years later, still not talking. Doctor says, "How is this possible? He is hearing, his ears no problem, this must be in psychology." Little boy does not make sound to cough, to sneeze, to cry. She says little boy, nightmares, holds mouth open like screaming but no sound. My cousin Nasser gives this woman money for son going to new doctor. He says thank you for tea, good-bye. Nasser promises I must tell you, "Fuck you." This is not only thing he says but most simple. Easiest to translate.

My brother, also I take many orders. I am soldier, too. I understand follow order, yes sir, yes sir. Follow order with hand on gun, finger on trigger. But also I understand rule of soldier. Man makes ghost, man keeps ghost. You cannot give your ghost for someone else's shoulders.

You are owner. My lovely. My brother. I send back to you.

(The lights fade on Ali. Elliot reaches into the envelope and pulls out the passport.)

ELLIOT: I can't get rid of this.
SHAR: What did it say?
ELLIOT: I can't get rid of it, Yaz.
SHAR: Whose passport is that?
ELLIOT: I can't get this thing off my hands.

(Shar takes the letter from Elliot and reads to herself.)

I took it to Jordan. I was like, "I'ma bury this here. Once and for all." I tried one night, after filming, but my whole body froze up. It felt like my blood was on fire. I could barely hold the shovel.

(Shar finishes reading the letter.)

SHAR: You never told me.
ELLIOT: You got a shovel, Yaz?

(Yaz goes to a closet. Shar takes the passport, looks at it.)

SHAR: This guy could be my cousin. His cheekbones. He could be my blood.
ELLIOT: I need a shovel.
SHAR: Story after story about the service and this is the one you leave out. Our son is marked. He's going to inherit this, our son, my son—
ELLIOT: Yeah, well that's how it happens. *(Violently grabbing the passport)* You think I learned this shit? It's in my fucking DNA!

SHAR *(To Yaz, heading to the door)*: It was nice to meet you.

YAZ: Don't you leave. You do not leave.

ELLIOT: This guy? Taarek Taleb? I knew he was a civilian. At first I thought it was a AK in his hands. Split second before I shoot, I'm like, that's a cricket bat. And then I pulled the trigger and took his face off. How am I supposed to tell anyone that?

(Yaz hands Elliot a trowel.)

YAZ: Here, Elliot. Best I can offer.

ELLIOT: Show me a spot in your garden where I can dig.

(Yaz leads them out to the backyard.)

YAZ: Right there. I've been meaning to pull up the avocado roots. They refuse to grow in Philly. But the soil there's good. The dirt goes down real deep.

(Elliot starts to dig but he trembles uncontrollably, freezes up. He drops the trowel.)

ELLIOT: Keep still, Elliot. Keep still. Come on. Breathe. Focus.

(His whole body trembles.)

Help me? Help me. Somebody help me!

(Yaz goes to help, but Shar stops her. Shar takes the trowel and begins to dig.)

YAZ: The dirt goes really far down. I found a penny that was a hundred years old down there.

(Shar digs and digs until she hits something hard.)

SHAR: I think that's the bottom.

(Elliot stands above the grave.)

ELLIOT: Taarek Taleb. It's been a long journey we've taken together, hasn't it? You and me, man. If I could give up my voice so your kid could utter one single word, I would do it. Or maybe I wouldn't. I don't know, man, maybe I'm not that brave. Taarek, may your little boy speak. Your son, my son. May both our little boys open their mouths and goddamn sing.

(Elliot pulls a pocket knife from his jeans, cuts himself, draws blood.)

SHAR: Elliot!
ELLIOT: Ahhhhhhh!

*(He lets a few drops fall onto the passport, puts the passport in the hole and begins to cover it with dirt.
    Lefty enters.)*

LEFTY: Mom?
YAZ: Lefty . . .
LEFTY: Your door was unlocked.
YAZ: Yeah. It was.
LEFTY: Can I come back home, mom?
YAZ: Sh. Come here.
LEFTY: Your door's been locked for a really long time. Do you forgive me?
YAZ: With every bone and bit of marrow. Do you forgive me?
LEFTY: The cement looks good. The cement didn't crack yet.

(Elliot finishes the burial.)

ELLIOT: There. Whew.

YAZ: Stay here, Lefty, I'll be right back.

(Yazmin exits into the house. Lefty fishes something out of his pocket: an old teddy bear. He gives it to Shar, a present.)

LEFTY: Don't be sad.

SHAR: Thank you.

(Yaz reenters with Agustín's cuatro, which has been repaired, and hands it to Elliot.)

YAZ: Hey little cheeseburger smile, your old music teacher left this.

ELLIOT: Agustín taught me that shit when I was five years old. And I forgot it all by the time I was six.

YAZ: Well start remembering.

(Elliot begins to play, plucking a few strings at a time, noodling around, having fun, laughing when he messes up.)

ELLIOT: I suck.

(He plays some more.)

Bo Diddley up in here. Carlos Santana shit.

(He plays some more.)

Just like a kid, right?

(Lights fade on the scene and rise on the Musicians. They sing a nostalgic verse about Puerto Rico.)

END OF PLAY

QUIARA ALEGRÍA HUDES's plays include *Elliot, A Soldier's Fugue* (Pulitzer Prize finalist); *Water by the Spoonful* (Pulitzer Prize for Drama); *The Happiest Song Plays Last*; *Yemaya's Belly* (The Clauder Prize); *26 Miles* and *Lulu's Golden Shoes*. Her work for musical theater includes the book for *In the Heights* (Tony Award for Best Musical, Tony nomination for Best Book of a Musical, Pulitzer Prize finalist), book and lyrics for *Barrio Grrrl!* and a new musical *Miss You Like Hell*.

Hudes's work has been produced on Broadway at the Richard Rodgers Theatre, Off-Broadway at Second Stage Theatre and 37 Arts, and downtown at Page 73 Productions. Her work has been seen across the country with premieres at the Goodman Theatre, Hartford Stage Company, The John F. Kennedy Center for the Performing Arts, Alliance Theatre and Miracle Theatre Group. Hudes's work has been translated into many languages, with productions in Armenia, Germany, Brazil, England, Japan, the Philippines and many other countries.

Other honors include a United States Artists Fontanals Fellowship, a Joyce Award, the Aetna New Voices Fellowship at Hartford Stage, and the Roe Green Award; with residencies at the Sundance Institute Theatre, The Eugene O'Neill Theater Center and New Dramatists.

March 16, 2014 was named "Quiara Alegría Hudes Day" in the City of Philadelphia. Mayor Rahm Emanuel declared April 27, 2013 "Quiara Hudes Day" in Chicago.

Hudes studied music composition at Yale University, earning a BA, and later received an MFA in playwriting from Brown University, where she studied with Paula Vogel.

She now lives in New York with her husband and children.